all violet

01 02 03 04 05 21 20 19 18 17

Caitlin Press Inc.
8100 Alderwood Road
Halfmoon Bay, BC V0N 1Y1
www.caitlin-press.com

Text and cover design by Vici Johnstone
Cover artwork by Michael Pittman
Printed in Canada

Caitlin Press Inc. acknowledges financial support from the Government of Canada and the Canada Council for the Arts, and the Province of British Columbia through the British Columbia Arts Council and the Book Publisher's Tax Credit.

 Canada Council Conseil des Arts
for the Arts du Canada  BRITISH COLUMBIA ARTS COUNCIL · Funded by the Government of Canada | Canadä

Library and Archives Canada Cataloguing in Publication

Rivera, Rani, 1981-2016, author
    All violet / Rani Rivera.

Poems.
ISBN 978-1-987915-55-6 (softcover)

    I. Title.

PS8635.I9433A62 2017   C811'.6   C2017-904631-4

all violet

Rani Rivera

poems

DAGGER EDITIONS

Contents

Acknowledgments

Were it not for the resolve of Rani's kindred spirit — and my friend — poet Ruth Roach Pierson, we would not have sought what we later found: a trove of poems by Rani, which she had squirreled away, and which Rani's partner, Seth Blender, worked to salvage and resurrect from her old computer. Huge thanks to Seth for his diligence and unwavering love and to Ruth for her persistence and immense support.

Deepest gratitude to Jim Johnstone for his editing and arranging of these poems into a manuscript. Many thanks to Rani's poetry group, friends and fellow students from the English Literature programme in which she was enrolled at the University of Toronto, who encouraged Rani's commitment to poetry and critiqued an early version of this manuscript — Christen Thomas, Lo Bil, Eve Christie, Hyam Hameed, Caley Moore, and Catherine Sweeney — and to Christen Thomas and Lo Bil for close-reading, and suggesting changes to, the final draft. A special debt to Lynn Crosbie, Rani's poetry teacher and friend, for nurturing her gift for poetry and guiding her along the way.

Finally, many thanks to Rani's publisher, Vici Johnstone of Caitlin Press, who readily accepted the manuscript for publication, impressed as she was with its contents on first reading. And to my family — Rani's dad, Joe, and Rani's sisters, Jenny, Patricia Kim and Isobel, as well as to other relatives and friends, for their love and care.

Patty Rivera, on behalf of Rani Rivera (May 7, 1981 – August 3, 2016)

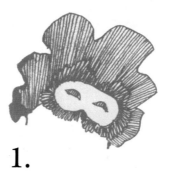

1.

ALL VIOLET

I used to think
verandahs were a construct for contentment —
instead I'm here
extrapolating on the reversal of repute.
50 years from now,
Jilly's on Queen and Broadview
will receive from future Torontologists
on a pretentious but never watched
literary newsmagazine
vis-à-vis a red-flamed editrix
having settled herself appropriately
in a brown leather club chair
kissing faux mahogany shelving
hiding a deficiency of real gilt-edged books,
but still standing and making do
with a room full of interns.

It's enough for a person to say
they've done it,
acquired national opinion rights
on the precise amount of cheese
and study needed
for poutine and Stendhal.

Charming the dress socks off
the resident poetry-loving investment banker
just enough to reward me a fat cheque
and another 500-print run.

Ingratiate myself to book club admin groupies
by owing a big thanks
to incest, milliners and Sioux Lookout.
Warrant a cropped likeness
of my insulated, too-big-for-my-snowpants head
drawn beside a weekly column
in the Arts section of one of the dailies.

Make a dark-chocolate-munching émigré of distinction
fall off his chair in round-bellied laughter
at yet another awards dinner.

Forget what CC and soda taste like
on a budget.

Take in a mangy stray and call her Maurice.
Show her off at the Jazz Festival
and be extra careful she doesn't get stepped on.
Write a poem about love, jazz and Maurice, and how she's
so cute, I could eat her.

NEW

Smitten has the same first intonation
of a Scandanavian man
in love, and his Helga beholden.
A state of disrepair and bondage,
irrevocably seduced by
stanza after stanza
of girls in bathtubs in pictures,
boy-men in suburban dreadlocks
and '70s two-car garages.

That pull of flesh
prepubescently porous
and wrinkled.

But not, not hard.

Not hard like smack
and the morning weather guy.

Not as hard as when I look at you
and see my disappointments.
Configure and caress
what I don't care for.
Tickle your knobby knees
with a finger
that's half your age.

Slip my tongue in between
gap-toothed breaths
during a noxious rock opera
of failed attempts
and drug-fuelled tumescence.

Immolation

"I have scars," she said. And I
looked at her, disbelieving.

This thing.

She lies in the comfort of train wrecks
and the company of men. I'm sure.

This minx.

Offers up valium
and dances, uproariously.

I look at her eyes
and they say nothing,

obviously.

I think them empty like mine.

APARTMENT HUNTING

Straight female, 26, seeks female friend to go out Saturday nights
for dinner, movies, hard rock shows and amusement parks.

She's a liar. I'm 98% positive I've seen that ad in *Women
Seeking Women*. But I can't begrudge her,
She might be from Sudbury or London
and feel lonely in the city.
But I know she's a liar —
she's been 26 for three years.
I don't know what's more frightening,
that she puts an ad out every week or
professing a love or hobby, mind you,
for amusement parks.
I've decided,
she is from Sudbury.

Personal ads get me off
amuse and inspire
drawn-out predictions
and quick judgments
of people's lives in 3 lines.

Take the aforementioned straight 26 yr. old female
To me it reads:
bull dyke not into the scene,
probably obese and works in computers.
Simply because we assume tech people are bored
and need to on occasion, "rock out"
and roller coasters just might be their bag.
The ad's lack of success suggests
a weight problem due to the fact
people are petty and don't like to befriend fat people.

My favourites are the personals in the *New York Review of Books.*
It's full of scruffy yet stately retired professors
and gin-soaked DJFs (divorced Jewish females)

into gallery hopping and Chet Baker.
I'd much prefer dry wit and good grammar over
a 22 yr. old male looking for females 18-60.

They're supposed to be a last resort
après-Friendster for the 20s-set
and for those too smart for J-dates and Jew-dos
but still hopeful, despite that
even after a fatwa
Salman Rushdie divorces his wife
and hooks up with a model.
She writes
nonetheless for *Vogue*.

Would Tristan search for Isolde this way?
Would we jump off a cliff to reunite with a dead lover?
Would we bring back the dead so
Richard Burton could marry Liz Taylor one last time?

There's no searching for the other half that makes us whole.
We're independent. We are whole.
But there is still a part of us that
shudders and misses what we once lost.
Nostalgic songs sung by big-hair bands
and the acceptance, however ludicrous and childish it may seem
that *November Rain*
tells it like it is,
as well as providing sweaty pubescent boys
a prolonged ass-groping session
under the disco ball in a suburban gymnasium.

People have to eat dinner.
There are some grown-ups willing to withstand
obnoxious teenage rockers with bad B.O. for a really good band.
And show me one person who doesn't love funnel cake.
Here's hoping she finds a masochist with a penchant for long lines.

NIGHT AND DAY

I'm getting off the 501 streetcar
and stomping my big, black boots into the sidewalk.
Surprisingly, my posture is perfect,
unburdened by a knapsack full of poems
and one vintage men's Burberry trench coat.

I'm heading home on Queen West West
in an asymmetrically zippered coat
and a Northbound Leather shopping bag in tow.
Carrying war wounds and forgotten accessories.
Feeling confident, cocky even, assured.

Even after it occurs to me I've never even considered
daylight before.
Relegated mornings to that dead air
occupied by
waiting for coffee to be made for you
while Cole Porter sings the blues away.

Sends your lover away.

Mornings are anoxic and pure,
full of phatic lovers and shared baths.

I'm seated at a new dining table
you salvaged from the street
and my bottom is cozy on a once-white chair
now a sunburnt polypropylene
and showing that sickly pallor of disease.
I'm trying to believe that I will remember this night
as a pleasant evening of tea and innocuous banter.

Blocking out
that after pushing aside
our worn Cohen vs. Dylan debate,
I ask to use your bathroom

and find a tin cup of makeup brushes by the sink.
A full set.
Professional even.

There's a loofah sponge in the shower
and I'm livid.

Angry that my mother never warned me
to stay away from
men in leather pants
who wear metallic nail polish
better than I ever can.
From men who tell you:
"you smell like bamboo and freshly cut grass."
From men who trek all the way to Scarborough
to find tiny D-rings to make your 4-inch stiletto boots
look couture.

I'm getting off the 501 streetcar,
feeling confident,
cocky even, dammit
assured.

Elizabeth Bath(ory)

Lately I've been wondering if I'm old enough
to start using eye creams,
and have decided resolutely to start budgeting
for botox injections before I'm thirty.
They say that cosmetic acupuncture works best
at the preventative stage rather
than when the signs of aging have already set in.
I guess it's a thin line between paying
someone to stab your face full of poison
and relaxing in a bath drawn from the blood of local virgins.

But I question the choice of your victims.
Does peasant stock really make for a heartier brew?
Wouldn't there be a greater chance of disease and how can
impoverished diets render the desired emollient effect?

You might have considered picking off
the fat ones with pretty faces.
Girls who eat all their sisters' pastries
and take meandering strolls on suitor-less nights.
From an economical standpoint there would have been
less bodies needed for bloodletting
and one less mouth to feed for her family.

But as we grow weathered by time
the price of vanity becomes sound investment.
The more NASA scientists, diamond grains and caviar
concocted in the brew, the more we believe
we can capture that elixir of youth and once again
revel in its frivolities and naïve assurances
of achieving a 22-inch waist without the aid of a corset
and nursemaids. Expect the slew
of gentlemen callers to never end.

So it was expected that this quest would take you
to seek out aquiline profiles and lofty foreheads.
Even predictable that you would realize topical agents
don't work as well and as quickly as oral tonics.
Any good alchemist could have told you that.

I would have told you to stay out of the sun
and don't marry a man you don't love.

Retreat

Mark was the first one to speak at the centre. The first one to break the cardinal rule of observing absolute silence. He had snuck in a couple bars of dark chocolate. The kind you buy at gourmet cafés for five bucks apiece. He told me later that he had noticed a certain sweet smell in my hair after we left the train station to join the others.

"So how many smokes you got?"
"Well, that depends on what you have to trade," I said.

We snuck away after afternoon asanas to take in the scenery and negotiate the terms of our illicit goods. He decided four squares of 75% cocoa for two cigarettes was a fair deal; after all, we were going to be there for ten days and it seemed prudent to ration out the smuggled excess we came there to escape.

He told me later he had been a lawyer for the past ten years and had recently become so disillusioned by the corporate world, he decided to take a sabbatical and find some semblance of meaning in his life. I looked at him the same way I looked at my sister's friend Dave when he told me he was leaving for Thailand to volunteer for an AIDS organization but didn't actually have to touch the people.

Each time we bumped into each other in the common room, he would find some way to accidentally touch me. He started placing his yoga mat directly behind mine, and grunted heavily after a particularly strenuous pose. Commented to the yogi, since he was the only one we were allowed to speak to, that his hamstrings ached after downward dog and asked if he was allowed to retire early to his room to rest.

So it became a daily routine for us, strolling the grounds solemnly before dinner until we faded out of plain sight to savour his sweets and my smokes. Joined the others in the dining room for brown rice and beans, both of us conspiratorially full. On the second-last day, I had only one cigarette left and he still had half a bar of chocolate. He asked to kiss me instead. And I let him. I don't know if it was out of sheer boredom or my lifelong addiction to good chocolate.

But nine days of observing almost complete silence, twice daily yoga practices and endless hours of meditation will make even the most earnest adept crazy. Maybe it was some kind of twisted foreplay, extended to ten days of unsought solace and horny sugar and nicotine highs.

After our last communal meal, our guru brought around a donation basket for the centre. Any monetary amount or simple thanks would suffice. Karma was the lesson we were supposed to have learned. Our own and how everything affects everyone at some point. We were finally allowed to speak and Mark asked me why I had really come to the retreat, while slipping me his business card. I told him I had just lost a lover and needed some peace, some time on my own, and placed his phone number in the karma basket when it finally came my way.

GIRL (INSTRUMENTAL)

if I've got to teach you about the hook,
you've got a lot more listening to do…

I said: don't go into that barn, yeah
hoo-hah hoo-hah
down by the water
the earthquake is making the house shake
Cupid grabs a pistol and shoots straight for the heart

he fed me fine food
he gave me shiny things
but it can't be man if it doesn't smoke
the same cigarettes as me

is this desire?
travelling without moving
just like a woman
your arms are calling out
just spread, spread for me
lay across my big, brass bed
I love the way you move
like this, Anna

but I'm already somebody's baby
I am 17 going on 18 and I'll take care of you

my magic 8-ball tells me just what I should do
will it tell me: yes or no?
will it tell me: stop or go?

why don't you just bloody well grow up?
you just sulk

oh baby c'mon, baby c'mon, baby c'mon

save it pretty mama
I'll chase the blues away
it's time to harvest the crust in your eyes

give me one good reason not to do it
I've seen the movie, I've seen what happens
that blue-eyed girl became blue-eyed whore
with her fog, amphetamine and her pearls
with a little help from my friends
how can you lie here and think of England
when you don't know who's on the team?

she was sweet 16, baby, beauty queen
she breaks just like a little girl
living on ice cream and chocolate kisses
she's got leather boots and suede
she goes down her on her knees and prays
but two turntables alone don't make it blend
everybody's scared of this place
they're staying away
your little house on memory lane

somebody's spoiling these women
the other woman finds time to manicure her nails
the other woman keeps fresh-cut flowers in each room
she will listen to me when I want to speak
about the world we live in and life in general
I want more, some more and then some

lilac wine is sweet and heady
the drugs work hard until they tire
I know my place, hate my face
I know how I begin and how I'll end
strung-out again
please don't let on that you knew me, when,
in an attempt not to leave out anybody,

I was tempted to leave out everybody
ease myself into a bodybag
I fall to pieces

Oh My Golly!
Bela Lugosi's dead
undead undead undead

Jane says
it's called a heart
ah, go fuck your pain away
this is not my life
you can be whoever you wanna be on a record
it's just a fond farewell to a friend

she said, "I want my freedom"
rise and shine, my sister

All in together now.

SHEET MUSIC

My mistress lies in exile on the moon
accompanied by a flock of ravens
I sent her a year before.
Summoned by gilded trumpets
at dawn,
she rises,
walking barefoot
through deep craters
and over shallow ponds.
Sometimes,
if the weather should suit her,
she might climb atop
a sleepy hill
to recite, practice, rather
the night's conversations with the sky
go over the usual pleasantries
and necessary appeasements
with the politeness and ease
of a routinely predicted rainfall.
Subdue her visitor
with a few teasing remarks
along with one or two witticisms
nothing too profound
just insightful enough to pore over
a few minutes
any longer than that
would raise the suspicions of the ravens
and cause the trumpets to stop.
By then, with a lift of her skirt
and a dance of her eyes,
she will bid me *adieu*
with a peck on my cheek
and murmur and sigh
in several foreign tongues
and with one ethereal gesture
lower her veil

striking hard at my heart
with brutish consonants
and the softest vowels
she will be gone,
as abruptly as the centuries
it took for her to come.

A PERFECT NIGHT
after Lou Reed

Burrowed far beneath the hairline
lies an elephant in the cross,
bespectacled and dreadlocked,
glistening with fifties pop
sensibilities
and cum strewn all over my leather.

Dousing our lamentation (of things)
with oil-soaked cloths
and miniature waterfalls, cascading
off-casted
glances
and shallow reservoirs of
the harvest's drunken catch.

Reeling in a certain sort of sorrow
metamorphosed into song

while

High on curious pills
from new strangers and
almost old lovers.
Circling a cavalcade
of old-school theatrics
and circus bumper cars.
Histrionically appealing
to the vicious
set of
faces, ennobled by
noses looking downwards,
judging
the coke to be as shitty
as our nostrils
deem it to be.

Conversation stunted
and pregnant with wood-locked
pauses
laden with scrupulous armour and
decorated with the requisite nostalgia
infidelity instructs.

Chock full of tears and
caricatures of first 'staches,
offering up bouquets of rue,
slick with the missed intentions
of an accidental gander
at a laundry room fuck.

Fresh from the purview
of a proprietorial promenade of
spouse and stroller.
Selling acts of seeming devotion
onto 12-inch vinyl, spinning
a tale of shaky knees and
well-aimed spit into the palm
of your hand.

Ready to leave
a heart stricken,
splayed anew.

2.

A Dereliction of Line

All I see now
are tuck shops full of ginsengs,
the preliminary "g" pronounced hard
and false by a friend who thought
me fearless.
Announcing gutturally, it's time
to clear the detritus,
too many hours have passed
tableside over a paltry purchase
she's spent and the lights are giving way.

One red
two black

starts a lazy, exquisite corpse,
lying unfinished in a haze
of the recognizable smoke and scent
of hard-topped construction cut
with digestives and filler.
Inclined to rush out
with trusted PIN codes and
newly acquired phone numbers.
Quashing old allegiances
and established sponsorships of
rehabilitated behaviour.

Drag Queens with a Side of Mash

I told you from the get-go
it was all just research.
You laughed, then propositioned me
to foils at dawn with your pinky finger,
substitute the sharp, metal blade
for your unwavering airs,
cede conventional weaponry
to my upright pen.
"I will give you that," he said,
before lifting those long dancer legs
sky-high
off the bed.
"Airplane ride?" he asked,
as if it was a lazy morning
query of sugar with my tea.

My memories are distilled
in a bottle of fine Russian vodka,
smooth to taste at first, then leaving
a dangerous bite in my palate,
whether it's gulped down heartily in the Caucasus
or seeped in ennui with a tart lemon garnish.

Your childish habit of falling asleep on the can
with picture books of Wellington and all things military
will bring us to Pimblett's for Thanksgiving dinner,
where the walls are covered with royals and your beloved general,
and littered with church bazaar teacups and mismatched chargers.
We will sit and chat pleasantly with British expatriates
and listen greedily and bright-eyed
when the owner cajoles us with stories
of his penchant to do the Queen in drag.
Sadly, he will leave us in his nubbly, wool cardigan
and sell his haven of sitting rooms and queens
later that year.

It is neither meat nor drink
but still requires an excess of both
when parrying indie pop vocals
and indulging in the dark.

Stranded in your hot, sticky room,
we will be at our happiest, our most civil,
when a blackout floods the city
and we go exploring the streets with a flashlight,
joining likeminded strangers for a quick and dirty dip
in an outdoor pool.

Assuaging your loss
of what a waste the two turkeys you bought on sale
were now
rotting together in your freezer.

We will go home and assess that they are beyond saving,
and fuck
until the lights come back on.

SOME FACTS, TRUTHS AND DECLARATIVE SENTENCES

Roy Boy is a rock star.

After Roy Boy sings/plays he feels his chances of getting laid are high.

Last night, he could have had a harem.

Roy Boy thinks about sex, a lot.

Barb is beautiful.

She sings beautiful jazzy numbers about drunken funerals, love at night and interesting times, to Rob's guitar accompaniment.

Bear is my girlfriend.

Sometimes she lets me sleep over.

Addie used to be my girlfriend, but she is far away now.

I miss her.

QUARTAN

*"I work with pictures and words because they have the ability to determine
who we are and who we aren't."*
—*Barbara Kruger*

Dougie says he can get better pot than Tommy.
We head out to South Parkdale, leaving Tommy's crackwhore behind.
Dougie tells me he's an electrician by day and only helping me out.
Tells me this is where I should have went in the first place,
that I shouldn't have trusted his cousin Tommy,
and I keep repeating to myself, "It's just like high school,"
knowing the outcome beforehand.
My sixth sense seething
from another rip-off
and guilty images
I've made in my head,
about what that crackwhore looked like
before she acquired the requisite stereotype.
Hustling in Parkdale,
not knowing that if it was a decade ago,
before the overpriced vintage shops
and bobo lounges,
I would have clocked her right in her face,
along with her boyfriend, cousin, uncle
god knows who else.

I go home to my bachelor apartment
just in time
for Peter, my neighbour
to bring home muffins from the Country Site Café.
Failing to ask in my drunkenness
if it was the resident moustachioed lady who served him.
Realizing, ironically
we're the fucked up
version of *Friends*.
Leaving our doors and fridges open.

But in our case,
it's either Stoli, Valium, pot
or strawberries.

Peter and I pick through our fraudulent drugs
and I say fuck it,
and smoke the pine leaves.

Leafing through his portfolio and worrying about the girl upstairs,
I find an oily, muscle-bound Trinidadian man
and ask him to draw it for me.
Ass up.

I think about that old lover
who left a ruddy, brown leather yoke in my apartment.
Appropriated from one of those old-man sports bars
right before our first platonic argument
over eggs and sausages at Dufferin Gate.
Think he could sell it on Ebay or to one of his dirty friends.
And pathetically think it would be one more reason
he could come over.

Initially, I thought it was part of a saddle,
but the girl upstairs informs me it's a yoke for cattle.

I'm hick, she tells me. Trust me.

She's sitting in my smoke-pit quarters
after I come home from another boring binge
and we munch on pizza and she fills me in
on where she's been the past couple of weeks.

Tells me she's been craving carbs like a motherfucker.
And that's what happens on anti-psychotics.
She's quite slim and hopes the extra weight

will be put on evenly, showing me the beginnings
of a pot belly on her 5'10", 120-pound frame.

"My parents have a horse farm in Lincoln, Ontario."

Her bratty little sister got ten ponies for her birthday.
Poised and perfect on a filly
and well-versed in dressage, jumping, English, Western,
rearing and breeding.

The girl upstairs confides to me
that she felt out of place in Art Therapy,
with the helmet-clad and strapped-down schizos.
Even though her fear of the Freemasons out to get her,
got her in there in the first place.
She figures she's just going to take her drugs
for a month and see how she can handle it on her own.

I tell her to simply do what she feels is best.
But make sure to take her meds.

She proposes an outing for the two of us,
before we get evicted and lose touch.
To get out of this city and visit the farm.
She'll make sure her sister's out of the way,
and we can just ride.

BENDER

There's a tree out there in the suburbs
my mother once wrote a poem about.
How we, or rather, she, had to get a cabbie
to measure the distance from the main street
to the corner I crashed into.

Not caring at that juncture
if I had woken the tree's keepers.
Or if they had children,
and how they would react in the morning
to see their front yard smothered
in police tape.

I imagine that there will be two of them.
One girl, one boy.
Hiccupping from their poached eggs and bacon,
excited with the prospect of telling their buddies
of how a misadventure had suddenly struck them.

Maybe they didn't even like the tree.
Maybe the boy kicked at it when his
mother told him it was time to go inside.
Maybe the girl scrawled her initials and
her elementary school crush into it.
Stabbed a heart around their love
with a pocketknife borrowed from her brother.

CICATRIX

I'm sitting on the floor at the Rivoli,
incapacitated by too many
double gin and tonics
and a wee toke of weed.
The woman on stage is sitting down as well,
cross-legged and masking her face
with indie-rock tresses.

I tell a friend I can't get up
because I'm enthralled,
and am afraid my red lace panties will show
if I try to stand up.

The woman on stage sings: " I hear fire…"
and even as my vision is hazy
I decide she is the most beautiful creature I have ever seen.

I had given her a good luck pat on the hip
prior to her set and hope
I haven't jinxed her.
Didn't know if our brief introduction
merited an innocent, girly slap on the ass.

I have a habit of getting trashed
and picking at people's bits.
Replacing my own compulsive skin-picking
for drunken slut-tease entertainment.

I saunter out for a cigarette with a cloudy confidence.
Talking to strangers and people whose faces
I recognize, but can never recollect
the next morning.
And somehow everything seems familiar.

And I don't mind,
that this city has almost eaten me alive.
Left a cartography of scabs and scars
running from my neck
all the way down to my feet.
Left people wondering where I escaped to,
why I wear long sleeves in the summer.

Where I live

I'm in love with Isabelle Huppert
but she doesn't know it yet.
She's oblivious to the fact that I can't pull off
peg-legged trousers
and can't for the life of me
sway saucer-eyed and wistful
to hybrid jazz-rock and transatlantic funk.

As much as I purse my lips
around clove-tipped cigarettes
with lovelorn determination,
my sleight of hand reveals
a predilection towards stout British beer
and whisky-eyed girls.

I'm not ready
to invite her to my pied-a-terre
on the outskirts
of Montparnasse for a glass or few
of Canadian rye.

I'm afraid she'll think it
provincial of me, much too facile an affair
to attempt a translation
of Hope Sandoval's lyrics and parse through
the hidden innuendoes and ethereal intonations
in her voice. Theorize about
the possibilities of dysphoric love and her victims.
Perhaps posit a muted hormonal firework display,
foreshadowing the advent of
mid-eastern American womyn festivals.
Finally acknowledging,
with a recycled paper and wood booth,
that some of us appreciate the alliterative
effect of a good spanking.

I could amuse her with anecdotes
and planned one-liners
about my misspent youth above
Shakespeare & Co.
Trundle incoherently past Peanut Plaza,
cement playgrounds and
the forgotten Spadina bus.
Isabelle, I think, would look on and listen politely,
as if preparing for a role
in an upcoming North American movie.
Memorize the exact creases in my makeup
when I share the schematics of building snow forts and
snow toilets in the guest parking lot at Vic Park and Finch.

Glean over the half-truths
when I spill my secrets over café au lait
and imagine what I've tactfully left behind
in unpacked boxes littering
my barely-christened Queen Street apartment
slated for demolition.

Impose on her the principle of superposition,
crosscutting strata tucked under my bed,
grounding balloon-a-grams from CAMH
inviting me to go to group.

But, with my eyes aslant
and predictably downcast

I'll tell her
that I've left it all
behind.

Confessed my fears
of being outed
at *Take Back the Night,*
and have decided

that moving eastwards is best.

It's where the sun rises,
becomes a child again.

It Only Matters When You've Got Something to Lose

Lila sits down on our dilapidated futon,
owning the room with her promises of yet more crack,
and pulls out the most intricate delivery system
I've ever seen.

Bragging that this maze-like cylindrical mess of glass
and chemistry is the one-up.
The best way.

Seventeen and still beautiful.
She sleeps on the streets and shows it.
It's funny how people can look so differently
in the daylight.

Lila sells her subway tokens to Dave,
like the rest of the welfare runts
littering the corner with the same stories
and lies she makes herself believe.

She is smart and knows it.

I look at her enviously,
unable to taste the kind of freedom
she throws away so cavalierly.

We talk of music. Frantically.
Nervous that she won't share.
Applaud her knowledge of a Tom Waits record
and his use of vignettes.

I know he thinks the same as me
and is surprised she even knew of the word.

She plies tales of car accidents, in multiple, and
the calming consistency of woe
that only regular doses of Dilaudid can fix.

He looks, I think, as if he wants some now.
I can only guess the relief of this camaraderie,

and wonder jealously if he wants to fuck her.

We welcome indigents and excess.
Little girls gone astray.

Wanting some roof to lie
under a while.

And we fleece them.
Thinking we're out-hustling the hustle.

The dealers come and go,
raising an inch of an eyelash
at the company we keep.

What is the appropriate response
to a teenager chiding you?

These girls, shrouding themselves
in oversized sweatshirts from The Stop.
Hiding, in vain,
the womanhood that betrays them.

The leverage they keep not.

How Not to Become a Homicidal Ex-Lover

First and foremost, stop with the bad writing made in bad lighting.
Then, unhook your computer, modem too.
Livejournal stalking may be legal now
but before you know it, government pigs will be knocking down
your door,
accusing you of conspiracy to commit murder and domestic terrorism
Force you to confess that the club you joined wasn't the I Hate AriClub©
but an underground cellblock
when your blog entries detail the simultaneous bombing of all goth
bars on Queen West.
Or at least, close them down for serving 18 yr. old trollops.
Stop dreaming in Kurosawa red.
Make do with self-help books and angry girlie rock lyrics.
Take advantage of that sudden burst of energy and hit the gym.
Not to look good when, by chance, you bump into that infidel on the
streetcar
but to avoid diabetes and hypertension.
Drink shots of wheatgrass daily to detoxify.
This will be a suitable replacement for Stoli and JD.
Remind yourself that vodka makes for bad decisions,
that's how you got here in the first place.
Don't switch teams out of vengeance, you'll only end up
breaking another girl's heart.
Chassé wine and kickball-change yourself into a pottery class.
Mold and sculpt a phallic ashtray to pound your cigarettes into
in disgust.
Forget altruism and volunteer in a soup kitchen.
It will make you feel better and leave you with a sense
that you smell better too, even look kinda hot.
Get dolled-up and slutted-out and hit the bar scene.
Flirt with the prettiest, most detached male specimen.
Order the most expensive drinks and put them on his tab.
Leave with the shyest, most common, introverted corporate geek
clad in khakis and ironic retro sneakers.
Ditch him in a cab heading west, two blocks later.
You have a headache. It can't be helped.

Clean out your apartment, but don't throw away his things.
Sell them.
Embrace celibacy for a while, treat and entertain her like an out-of-town friend.
Visit your mother and tickle her big, cushy belly.
Use this as a template of what not to become.
Don't invest in shrinks and aroma-quackery,
they're bad for your allergies and your budget.
Instead, learn how to read tarot cards and fix it so
you'll be rich, beautiful and successful.
And for fuck's sake, throw out those black candles.
You've got to face it. The curse didn't work.
Your karma's fine.

3.

Just Some of You I've Known

They ask, always and inevitably

"Where have you been these past five years?
What's new with you?"

"I fell in love with a man. A crackhead
to be precise,

        and he loved me too."

The dog did it for me. Was the last
string undone to tie me back up.
His age, his wares, became some baby bonus
unexpected.

       I saved it up all for him

There were the others in between, and before,
then during. An act of reprisal
committed flagrantly, a pity
fuck turned all year round.
Who was worse off and unattended
is still up for debate. We
ruined each other, beautifully.

An electron pair, sidled up against
each other in feats superhuman
and disgusting.
No amount of drugs
could anticipate the reciprocity
of time suspended.
The cruel intimacy
of our courageous hatred.

Even when we were dying
I still believed you.

Held out for the goat farm
and magic vegetables, summoned
fantastically from some unnatural earth.

I dressed you with childlike whim
and 70s punk pomp.
Drew satisfaction from your
funeral parlour onstage.

You let me.

Yet even when you walked down the streets
alone, feet uncertain and shuffling eternally,
stripped of that manic direction
of the past 11 days awake
and wired on endless streams of
bad Japanese porn and dodgy stimulants,
I could still find you
and wanted to hold your hand
as if it were my own.

You were a rat that glowed in the dark,
fastened precariously with a safety pin
on a frayed collar. Delightfully
unhinged and dangling.

How do you explain away
dryly and wittily worded conclusions?
This conclusion? Our end?

Do I start with those awful orange walls
that seemed to go on forever?
That murderous red ceiling? That stench we made?
The noise below?

This old dance
was never new.
Despite the change in instructor
our tune remained the same.
Repetitive and rocking,
reliably
in ferment,
until our legs gave up
and I couldn't walk any longer.

∞∞∞

He says to me,
"Leave the door open."
And I piss for him
across the hall, while he lies and watches
me from his bed. Observes the wiping
of my crotch without expression.
This sinister cowboy, goateed
and greying, finds pleasure in withholding.
I do what he says, slowly and with
affect. Careful not to look in his son's room
as I tread barefoot and
naked in this basement apartment.

We wake up finally and fuck
quickly.

Mid-afternoon,
I put on last night's clothes
and am left with one last instructive,
making sure it's all understood,
to never speak of this
to his ex-girlfriend.
It would break her
heart.

This one tells me his previous lover
won't play
tennis with him anymore.
She never liked the sport,
only did it to appease him.
Somehow he's dumbfounded
at her newfound honesty.
Resents the fact she played
with him at all.

This one is too big
for his britches. This one I like.
This philosopher-cook,
charitably endowed with an uncommon intellect
and a giant box of special condoms,
numbs my ears with his irrational
obsession with pizza.
I had never heard of the pizza makers' union
and wish that really I never did. I don't care
much for Lacan and his theories.
It's not that I don't find them valid
or interesting. It's just not relevant
to the situation. Who gives a shit
about the temperature of dough
and the mirror stage?
I have an intolerance
for wheat, and children,
especially babies,
bore me.

I just want you
to sometimes
put your cock in my mouth,
but mainly in my cunt,
then cuddle and call it a day.

The crazy one. The one whose mother woke me
to tell me he jumped off the roof
has stuck around.

Ingratiated himself into my periphery. Found others
more pathetic than he.
We avoid each other systematically
like a high school couple newly on the outs.

Though simple and thoroughly inconsequential,
he grates me. The dumb are usually honest.
And I believed him when he told me of how
he drove to Cherry Beach one day and screamed out
into the ether.
Couldn't fathom my history of hurt.
Shared my anger and hate for you.
False sympathy pains aside, I smiled genuinely
when he called in early morning, after having just left me
with his dog and promises,
with a premature declaration of love.

I should have known I would ruin
the city's mojo, as he put it,
that I would be the rotten catalyst (sic)
in his life that lured him off path.

We laugh at his threats of dragging my name through the mud.
Wonder incredulously, who says such a thing?
And you assure me that you will defend my honour. That I am
your very good friend.

Two others are broken, completely.
The way I like them to be, wallowing and sore.
Having been left by the one they loved.
These two are lost, and too tender to even bother with.
They are the far gone.

There was a collision of sorts
when I met you.
Your rabid eye latching onto the detritus
of a girl's first apartment.
The caked-on dishes left in the sink for a month
induced a manic offer to wash them clean.
But I didn't let you that night.

There was a coy straddle lying about, an offer
to ineffectually pounce on the grit
of the bottom of a bottle. The tail end of valiums
and vodka needed so desperately. Another fix.
Another time to try again and fail. Wake up
in the afternoon and say to oneself,
the day is already gone, why bother.

ooooo

One girl makes me so happy
when she covers her mouth with her hand
when she cums.

ooooo

Another remains so sweet and kind
I don't mind being a repeat guest star,
and seek their occasional comfort
when I need solace in obliteration.

ooooo

I should start with how breaking your heart keeps breaking mine.
Or the way your way of walking changed. Of how I felt pity for your
face.
Felt sorry for your eyes
and head of hair swooped preternaturally into a capital C,
ending with shoes you refused to lace up.
Constantly tripping and travelling
as if that last trip to the bar was a mistake.
My love, all our trips were a mistake.
You could not go on any more runs for ruin of us.

It feels like velvet
on a Sunday morning.

I lied to you beautifully and courageously.

Christmas even.

And I'm still unwrapping the contents
of another glassine bag
and falling
victim to this absurd ritual
of carving yet another life.

Told you,

you would always be mine.

4.

To Return to Heaven like a Stain

Darling,
don't you know
I'm old hat
at this?

I can stomp these boots
and smear my lips
with Russian Red
and sit on some fashionable
stone slab in Yorkville,
turning heads with argyle
and stripes together.
Block all this bullshit

new spring sun with
a pair of Jackie O's
and a Pall Mall cigarette.

Forget about yesterday.

Today I'm playing pretentious.
And I'm doing it beautifully.

My fuzzy yellow beret
is perched perfectly askance,
to hook would-be suitors in
good weather.

How easy it is
to walk away

from a stretch of fetal positions
and begging for benzos
behind electronic doors,

when I can do bohemian glam
so well. So well.

Aren't I brave to
read *The Phenomenology
of Anger* and be
inspired?

Abrogate! my citizens. I'm participating.

Today is a day
of foolishness and facades.

Perhaps tomorrow I'll wrap
a present,
then open it,
and find it to be the same.

The Oldest Profession in the World

Annie St. John
December 6, 1999
Strangulation

Danni Papeo
January 2, 2000
Pneumonia, complications of HIV

Moira
January 29, 2000
Car accident

Beth Goodwin
February 14, 2000
Homicide, gunshot wound to the head

Natalie Hussein
April 1, 2000
Breast Cancer

Riley Kitts
May 31, 2000
Complications during childbirth

Megan O'Shaughnessy
August 28, 2000
Internal bleeding from aggravated assault

Ruby Lopez
Oct. 14, 2000
Adverse reaction to anesthesia during breast augmentation

Kennedy Jones
Nov. 29, 2000
Suicide (self-inflicted lacerations to the wrist)

Anna Zamyatin
December 23, 2000
Hypothermia due to extreme weather conditions

Jane Doe
January 2, 2001
Drug Overdose (Heroin, Cocaine, Crystal Meth, OxyContin, Marijuana, Valium, Prozac, Zyban, Insulin)

Waste Case

He was there the first time
I begged for it.
Told me of how cocaine is like the tumult
of the rocking waves of the sea
and heroin is like landing on a sandy beach.
Or something like that.

And now, years later, both of us clean
and on the narrow end of surviving,
he's become a different sort of friend.
Confides to me of how he didn't like me
back then. That day I made my ex-lover
take the rent cheque back.
They don't really need it, I had said.
We did.

He thinks I'm slipping,
now. And I agree.
Wrote a song about me
and it's beautiful.
I show him a poem I wrote about my ex-lover.
His best friend.
And I like this exchange of art,
this nominal transaction of sadness.

But I can't fall for another 50 yr. old ex-junky musician.
I'm older now and don't have the heart.

Even after he tries to tackle some asshole
video-taping the infamous Jane Doe at a rally against rape.
There's a publication ban, he yells.
No violence, scream the women
behind us. My hero,
I think, three days drunk.

My hero, to listen to me wail all night.
Hiccupping and slurring from copious amounts of red wine.
From all those years of prolific cruelty and love.
My hero, to hold me and tell me that he ruined me.
My ex-lover. His best friend.

He thanks me for this new perspective.
Understands it all now.

And I stay silent
while we walk
through Chinatown and the fishes.
Points out his first bank
and I think it strange
to remember first accounts.
That cartoon bank book they give you
to teach you how to make your
first withdrawal and deposit.
To keep a balance and learn responsibility.
Fiscal or otherwise.

No, I meant the first bank I robbed.
Correcting me.
We laugh and I remember who I'm with
and what my life is not.

You're my buddy girl, he says.

And I look at him through the gleam of the spring sun
and the familiar stench of street and ardour
and say,

You're my buddy boy. Smiling.

BLANK GENERATION

Corky keeps circling around the block,
stopping every five minutes to ask,

"Is he here yet? What's happening?"

"*No, man.* He's not answering."

Roy is grim, cell phone at his ear,
pacing.

It's not looking good, and I can't
shake off this edginess.

Keep smoking. Keep waiting.

No one is talking to another.

We're all just chain-smoking,
trying not to look tweaked out while
we sit on some dirty bench
in that Kensington parkette.
Trying hard as hell
to not give in to this sketchy *mise-en-scene*.

We're all cool. Just a small group of friends
hanging out in the market,
relaxing in the twilight.

Every minute, every unanswered phone call,
every fucking time Corky drives by,
impatient, feels like murder.

Fuck. You gotta believe.

He's going to come any minute and
that will be the end of it all.

Right? Everyone will be happy
and relieved.

Drugs dealers are always late. It's their M.O.
Maybe he's a user. That'll make him more
fucked up. Less reliable with time
but more reliable in the long run.

Users are the best kind of dealer.
You know they're going to come through,
because just like you and me,
they have to score too.

We're all in this together. Waiting
not to die.

Come on. Pick up, so we can
pick up.

A couple of hundred dollars' worth of customers
and this kid is fucking
it all up.

He says he's on the way, but
he might as well say he's late because
he's the Queen of England.

I'm too busy with tea and crumpets, you motherfuckers.
You all have to wait.

He has to come through, I think.
I can't bear to do the other anymore.

I'm too young for this shit.

Keeping company with aged rock stars
turned professional addicts.

Woodstock was way before my time
and I'm not some half-naked girl on a horse
coming true
in your '60s psychedelic dream.

I'm just a girl who got into a little bit of trouble.

This all seems so right and familiar.
Like yeah, man, I've been working towards
this moment.

Always knew I would find out
eventually
what home felt like.

Wanted: Your Bad Karma

Broken mirrors, boots stepped on cracks,
shoelaces and all...
please don't send anything smelly though.

Torn-up love letters, sent or not,
E-mails trashed, and salt
kept hidden,
even after its volley
over your shoulder
proves to be unsuccessful.
A remnant of failed marks in Gym
and Art.

Your Art teacher requests a meeting with you
when you submit a piece laden
with syringes, uppers and downers,
on an open-faced sandwich
when you're supposed to depict
your kitchen.
Your cupboards.

What do you keep on hand?

Monk straps on black, mock-leather shoes,
polka-dotted excess material,
flared to oblivion
on too-baggy-for-your-frame jeans.

While trying to be more ethnic,
not in that belly dancing,
be-proud-to-be-brown kinda way
but be hard,
hip-hop gangsta.
Nothing shall faze you.

Pack up your heritage and leave it in Vic Park and Finch.
Collect the swatches of fabric and residue,
and configure your canvas
with the same zeal
you had when you stole from grubby, little hoodlums
playing bloody knuckles
on bare mattresses and white walls.

Take everything they've got.

Take Verlaine's bullet
from his pistol and linger awhile,
fondle cool beads of
evaporating suspension
in between raising a glass
after you
appropriate Apollinaire's *parapluie*
and taste that burn vodka makes
on cold-sored lips.

Sit in a confessional,
oak, cedar or
whatever fuckin' wood
you're supposed to kneel on
when you're guilty.

And tell,
please,
a white-collared man,
adjunct to the other world:
you've done wrong
and wish to repent

Change, simply
the colour of collars,
that thread of fabric
from muslin to black leather,
then ask for forgiveness.

GHOST NOTES

Fuck-Face City here I come
I want some brand new — decadent fun
          — Chris Houston, "Fuck-Face City"

This hat doesn't fit.

It's all morning and I'm alone again.
Brandi's leaving me, and I can't quit.
I bought her two bags Thursday night.
Her dealer's doling out some big brother
sibling-type confidences and the regular bullshit.

They don't care and they care.

Sometimes I see my mum and me waiting
for my older brother at the bus stop.
She yells,
"Where the fuck's your fuckin' brother?"
at me,
and I'm still looking up at her, little
and a bit
hairy for my age. It's lunchtime in August
and I'm always sweating.
"I don't know. He'll show soon. He promised, this time
he'll be good again."
She exhales like all the other mothers,
dumps her cigarette on the ground,
leaving the butt-end halfway lit,
still shining.

                    ∞∞∞

He turned off the television last night
and declared,
"Movie night's over, guys. See ya next time."

The first time
fingers found their way
up my legs, I didn't care.

The son of a bitch didn't even wash his hands. Didn't want me to
either.

"What are you doing down here, Brandi? Did you
get beat?"

His palms were so soft and foolish,
like piñatas knowing they're going to get hit,
breaking into candy and pavement.

"No, Dave." I brushed his hands away
that time.
"Oh, I see. You got diddled."

He gives me a kiss and takes off
his hat, laying it down on the glass counter like lilacs,
smashes his nose in between my breasts
and whispers,
"There's no one here, baby girl.
Go on, tell me
you're beautiful."

WAITING ROOM/PERSONALITY CRISIS

"Jesus? This is Iggy."
    —Iggy Pop

Giraffes are known to be tall
and elegant yet awkward.
And this is what this man is.
Solomon. King of kings.
Eats his meals like a wayward
falcon. His fingers move swift
like talons. Pick, pick
picking.

He is so thin I wonder if they ever
make it up to his lips.

Maria. Or Regla Maria,
lies in bed grieving,
relishing the tourniquet of stars
in her trashy magazines.
Waiting and singing, trance-like,
while alternately kissing her fake baby
and gossiping to her many friends
from the daycare about dildos
and how old so-and-so is now.

Such a cliché for an ex-jinetera.
I think I love her.

Her eyes have gone out.

I saw them glisten
briefly, when, as accidents happen,
we pass through the birthing ward
and Marian, our nurse and accompaniment
to trips to that outside world,
explains gently, that *these* nurses

are wary of mental patients.
Did you ever hear the one about that crazy lady
going to a hospital and kidnapping a newborn baby?
Just picked her
right up.

Maria and I are cigarette buddies.
Held hostage by some kind of bureaucracy
and hospitable concern.

Clinching to whatever air is there
to steal in this silence.

I can see Jason, handsome
and enfianced, through a small
slit in his curtain.

He came here like the rest.
Fragile, pronounced en francáis. For affect.

C'est triste pour la.

Drugged and beaten by
his roommate.
I imagine him naked and lying
on the street. Waiting for me.
What's his deal? Not really one of us, I suppose.
He seems so ultimately
straight, and gay
and together.

His fiancée is a cow.

She had to buy him new clothes
because, like the newly born or the dead,
he had none.

Heather looks just like her name.
Scraggly, red reeds of hair,
and hips so thin
you could sew her body
into one eyelet.

She is one of the lucky ones.
Waiting and sitting, quietly,
like some officious mouse spying
through a hole
for her methadone.

Ready to attack.

Her face reads: No Trespassing Here.

She seems nervy and I decide
not to like her.

There is always a turncoat in these parts.
Wrecked by her desire to heal.

Becca, the nurse, with her gaping
eyes and requisite inch of a chin
(Why are their eyes always so big?),
would be so sweet and suitable for her job
if not for her profound unsuitability.

Pyjamas for scrubs. Pick one.

We are not scared of *them*,
as Maria or Regla Maria's voices
insist. They shift, hourly
or daily? Still, we stay the same.
As if we had been here, always.

The word always comes with connotations
of peppermint hearts and cheap engravings.
The hopefulness of youth
and blue, blue skies skimming
against a perfect water.

Not the language of worn-out
brigands and the bottlenecked
highways of the disengaged.

Becca's doctor, according to her,
laid it all out: "He ain't never gonna come
back to you."

After watching Becca and her ex-husband
place tile after tile on the Scrabble board, piling up points
and silences on a hospital notepad.

Venice is Falling

I see a man,
stone-faced and tired,
in a Valium whirl.
Treadmarked and used,
doused and dug out from the coal.

Left-behind flat-footed croupiers,
standing out by the banks
with billfolds
and lonely countesses.

He's sinking,
and all the gondoliers
and Verdi, Puccini,
Sevillian barbers
can't muster the strength
to bring him into tow.

He sails with bright red flags,
polished wood, reinforced
with a neighbouring queen's army
and allegiance.

Yet, there he goes.

Singing a waltz,
slow and unencumbered.

FOR AN HOUR OR ALWAYS

I love them
broken and beaten badly,
pock-marked and toothless,
spent and riddled with rue.

I love them lying
with sleep in their eyes,
the sunlight curdling
in sweet bellies
heaving with the unrest of a few
too many.

I love them motherless
and taunted. Violent
and entitled.

I love them on fire. I love them on ice.

I love them hairy and unclean.
Hearts pierced and sagging.

I love them old. I love them new.

I love them mean.
I love them talking and talking.
I love them destructed and
pinned with little needles,
smokestacks of inconstancy.
Nailed to the wall and stuck on
with glue.

I love them dancing, dancing.

I love them withholding and
threatened with kisses.

I love them on top of me,
climbing.

I love them passionless and crude.
Spinning and wearing scratches
on their sleeves.

I love them long gone.

I love them picking apart
pieces to play. Deciding
what to learn by heart
and what to throw away.

I love them loving
other people. I love
them forgetting allegiances
and running away from battle.

I love them half in the ditch,
head cocked up with one arm flailing,
the other in my pocket.

I love them looking at me
and forgetting.

I love them when there is something to prove.
A position to assert.
Backed up and already impotent.

I love them facile and running.

I love them jumping off roofs.

I love them snarling,
and smiling without hope.

I love them fabricated,
mouths full of cotton.
Their syringes overflowing
with bullshit.
Pipes filled with nightmares
and oily schemes.

I love them poor and sweating
with every kind of sickness.

I love them withdrawing
from the world. I love them
leaving. I love them
awake and scornful.

I love them pretty
with their ugliness.

I love them all violet
and blue.

I love them charging.
Metamorphosing into steel
with a drop of a hat, to bid me *adieu*.

I love them panting and asthmatic.
I love them throats throttled,
hair long and bewired.

I love them blind
with rage, screaming
euphoniously in unkempt rooms.

I love them falling
down jerry-built stairs,
slamming face-first on their own floors.

I love them
believing in love,
its full assault.

I love them breaking
bottle after bottle
of homemade brew.

I love them needing
the persistence of tears.
The cruelty of kindness,
that disgusting embrace.

I love them gay
and unhappy.
Popular and forlorn.

I love them wounded
and bleeding,
propped-up and bandaged badly.

I love them dying and dying.

The already dead and useless.

I love them unchanged
and stuck in time, like vampires.

I love them trolling
for the same victims.
Finishing them off with the same refrain.

I love them
when they can't stand it.
I love them when they give up
and pack away my things,
thinking themselves to be benevolent
and brave.

A Revised Suicide Note

When I go out, I want to go out in a blaze of Japanese pop rock.
I'll get gussied up in a striped pink and white argyle sweater
and neon-orange knee socks.
I will sing my own revved-up rendition of some Moody Blues song,
karaoke style.
I will enthrall my mostly-white, middle-class audience
with frenetic dancing and shaggy hair.
I will wear my sailor scout rings on all my fingers
and intentionally display my proclivity
towards Sailor Mars and Jupiter,
wearing their insignias on both my ring fingers.
I will shout broken hip-hop slang when I forget the words,
then suddenly stop right in the middle of my set.
My band members will look on, not sure
if it's a gimmick or if something is actually wrong.
Is there something wrong with the mic
or is something amiss with the singer?
I will run to stage left and triumphantly return
with a cello.
It will be too big for me, and I will fall. People will gasp and
smile silent, open-mouthed giggles.
I will yell "no worries" into the mic and flash them
an all-purpose victory sign. All is saved,
for the moment.

No, scratch that.

I want to go out in a warble of
Patsy Cline and
an alcohol-level reading of cheap, but still
substantial, Chilean wine
with a copy of a Donovan record in plain view
to throw the cops off
when they trip over Braveheart Lion on the way to
the bathroom.

My little man will be tossed off my unmade bed, left
askew and occupied by last week's newspapers on the floor.

I'll leave a copy of *Bondage for Dummies*, signed
by Midori, fidgeting off my shelves.

My cops will look around
for evidence, motive,
and an artistically inclined rookie will stop
and peruse my Plexiglas-protected case
of old lighters,
wonder if my hanging Ikea shelves would
look good in his fiancée's new apartment.

I'm so tired that
I accidentally slip into the
tepid water of
my bathtub I cleaned, never.

I'll lose consciousness and get caught in the undertow
of giant bubbles because
I never learned to swim and
hot tubs are particularly bad for those with sensitive skin.

Aphrodite is said to have come from the foam of the waves
in the sea, and
Venus is my moon sign and
my cousin in Vanuatu is a cutter.

She's young, and slim like her mother.
One morning my aunt came into her room
to wake her up for school and found that
her daughter had something to show her.
Her mother, the doctor, promptly stitched her back up
and scheduled a psych appointment later that day.

I reached out to the moon last night and
found it wasn't there.
Sometimes I'm not so sure
if what I've said is true
to what I set out to be.

Nevertheless, I keep doing it.
Perennially patching up the
latticework left on my skin.
Picking myself up
from the dirt and
reminding myself that
people fall all the time.